Real Estate

:: Author ::

Vaishaliben Makwana

Assistant Professor

Government Arts & Commerce College, Kathlal

PUBLISHED BY

The New Era International Publishing House
HQ. At & Po. Chaveli., Ta- Chansma,
Dist- Patan, North Gujarat, India, Asia.
www.iphouseindia.com

First Publication: 24th NOVEMBER, 2015

Copyright: Author

(c) **Vaishaliben Makwana**

ISBN:- 978-1-51950-140-0

Price: Rs.800/- INDIA

$ 15 OUTSIDE INDIA

PUBLISHED BY

**The New Era International Publishing House
HQ. At & Po. Chaveli., Ta- Chansma,
Dist- Patan, North Gujarat, India, Asia.
www.iphouseindia.com**

Dedicated

to

my

Parents

Types of Real Estate Investors

Real Estate markets are extremely complicated. The price movements in this market are usually slow and difficult to come by. A major factor behind this is the type of investors who put their money in the real estate markets. Therefore, an understanding of the real estate markets has to be rooted in an understanding of the underlying participants as well as their motives. We will have a look at these factors in this :

Investment Motive

The most important feature based on which we can distinguish real estate investors is their investment motive. All investors buy real estate. However, not all of them do for the same reasons. Let's have a look at the three major categories of investors in the market.

- **Speculators:** These are the kinds of investors that should not be called "investors" in the first place. They give a bad name to real estate investing. This is because if you read their blogs and believe their claims, they will make a sophisticated operation like real estate investing sound like a no brainer. These are the people that claim to have made a million dollars in 4 years without any investment of their own simply by flipping real estate. The truth is that such results are almost never obtained. Real estate investment is an old school investment game which only pays off in the long run. Most of these speculators are either people trying to make a quick buck by selling their phony "surefire real estate profit strategy" or people who have fallen prey to these con men and are actually trying these phony strategies in the market! This category of investors was hard to find just a few years ago. However, of late, they have become a lot more common.

- **End Users:** This is the most common category of investors that you will find in the real estate market. Usually people who buy real estate are buying their own homes. They have the intention of staying in the house for decades. This changes their outlook towards the investment. These people do not look at real estate as a purely financial decision. They look at it as a lifestyle choice. This is because they have to stay in that house day in and day out. Hence, factors such as lifestyle amenities available nearby as well as the distance it takes to commute to work become extremely important. The demand for these kinds of investors can be predicted based on where their job locations currently are or are expected to be in the near future.

- **Long Term Investors:** Lastly, we have the long term real estate investors. Like the "flippers", these people too invest in the real estate market to make money. However, their decisions are not short term. They understand that real estate is a slow moving, illiquid kind of asset that steadily grows in value over a number of years. Many corporations are also present in the real estate investment business.

Degree of Control

The long term investor category can be further subdivided into two more categories. These categories are distinguished based on the degree of control they exert on the property in question.

- **Active Investors:** Some long term investors prefer to manage the property themselves. They are the ones who conduct the repairs, find the tenants and rent out their properties. Also, they may be actively involved in the property management process and may visit the property several times to ensure that no damage has been carried out by the tenants. Since they actively participate in the investing process, they are called active investors.

- **Passive Investors:** There are other long term investors which have the ownership of the property. However, they do not take interest in managing its day to day affairs. To do so, they either hire employees or they end up hiring professional real estate management firms. Since they play no role in maintaining the property, they are called passive investors. They just provide the cash flow for financing the property and make very few (if any) decisions regarding its management.

Legal Entity

Lastly, the type of real estate investors can also be distinguished based on the type of legal entity they are. Legal entity is important because it determines the amount of liability that a person has.

- **Individual Investors:** Most of the investors in the real estate market are individual investors. Individual investors have an unlimited liability. This means that if they undertake a mortgage on one house and default on it, their other assets can be liquidated to make good the loss.

- **Institutional Investors:** There are many institutional investors in the real estate market as well. These institutions usually finance themselves by issuing long term bonds in the bond markets. Since these bonds have a secondary market, they are very liquid and provide the investors with the ability to enter and exit the real estate market without any major hassles. While, in terms of number, individual real estate investors may outnumber the institutional investors, in terms of scale or volume, they are no match for the big corporations who invest billions of dollars in real estate investments.

Real estate market, like the other markets, is therefore complicated. It has various investor groups, who have different motives and based on the competition and co-operation between them, the real estate prices are set.

Real Estate Investing Myths

Amongst all investment options available, real estate is the one that buyers tend to get emotionally attached with. For this reason, people rationalize their emotional decisions with the help of many myths about real estate investing.

If one wants to avoid getting entangled in the emotional aspects of real estate investing and make financially sound decisions, it is imperative that these real estate myths be recognized and dismissed. **We will list down some of the foremost real estate investing myths and try to debunk them.**

Myth: Land is Scarce

The most common myth propagated by real estate salesmen and other proponents of real estate investing is that land is scarce. There is only a limited amount of land in the world. This coupled with the fact that the population of the world is increasing everyday gives credence to the conclusion that the land prices of the world will continue to rise perpetually since there will always be a shortage of land.

However, a look at the numbers will explain that this is not the case. Firstly, it is true that there is a limited amount of land in the world. However, technological development is making it possible to make more efficient use of this land. Studies have been conducted in this area and their conclusions state that even if the population of the world were to rise four fold, there would still be an abundant amount of land for all humans to survive and thrive!

Secondly, studies have also been conducted which state that the population of the world is about to stabilize. This means that the population growth era has reached its peak and now the number of people will remain more or less constant.

Hence, the "land is scarce and therefore precious" logic is nothing but the propagation of a myth!

Myth: Land Prices Always Go Up in Value

This logic is prevalent largely is developing economies which have witnessed unprecedented boom in the real estate sector in the past decade or so. The price of land in these economies has gone up 10 times in the past two decades. As a result, people in these countries have come to believe that the price of land always rises i.e. the real estate always goes up in value.

This is far from the truth. If one were to consider developed economies like Japan and the United States, one can find examples of real estate crashes where prices have dropped to the tune of 40% to 50%. In Japan, the prices have gone down and have continued to stay there for the better part of the last decade.

Hence, once again, "land prices always appreciate in value" is a mythical statement. Land prices are connected to many factors one of which is the well being of an economy in general.

Myth: Past Performance Predicts Future Performance

There is a common tendency amongst hopeful real estate investors to extrapolate the trends that were present in the property market in the past and create an extremely bullish future scenario. However, one needs to understand that the world has undergone a fundamental shift in the last decade or so. Business arrangements like outsourcing, free trade and cross border investments by multinationals had created an unprecedented boom in the emerging economies. The future does not apparently hold any such revolution in its offing. In case, no unexpected economic revolution fundamentally changes the economic paradigm, it is highly unlikely that the performance of the past few years gets repeated in the future years. Investors betting on a repeat performance are in for a rude shock!

Myth: Real Estate Investments Can Be Flipped Easily

This is not a very popular myth. However, before the subprime crisis broke out in the United States, stories of self made real estate millionaires who owe their fortunes to nothing but buying and selling real estate on borrowed money were common.

These bloggers propagated the virtues of flipping i.e. buying and selling real estate several times in a very short period. The idea was to book the profit arising from the price differential and converting it into cash. However, what these self-proclaimed gurus forgot to mention is the huge amount of transaction costs that are associated with any kind of real estate transaction worldwide. Therefore, the more properties you flip, the more transaction costs you incur. These transaction costs amount to anywhere between 2% to 5% of the price of the property in question.

Apart from the transaction costs, finding a willing buyer and negotiating a deal is a tedious and time consuming process. Flipping properties therefore causes immense drainage of time as well as resources and therefore should be avoided as far as possible.

Myth: Buying is Better Than Renting

Property buyers all over the world have an emotional connection with the real estate that they purchase. From traditional times, buying real estate has been considered the "adult" thing to do for a person. This decision has no financial backing and is rooted in the thinking that having a property to your name somehow makes one economically more secure.

However, if we consider the financial aspects this is clearly not true. There are some situations when buying is clearly the better thing to do whereas there are other situations where renting is the best option. The ideal thing to do therefore depends on a case to case basis. This rent vs. buy decision will be discussed in a later.

Real Estate and Money Supply

There is a direct relationship between the amount of money supply that is available in the system and the amount of money that finds its way into the real estate market. This is because real estate is one of the most preferred investment classes in the world. It is considered to be a safe haven and one of the safest hedges against inflation.

However, very few people are aware of the fact that real estate also ends up creating more money supply! This is because of the way the modern fractional reserve banking system works. The more real estate is created, the more mortgage loans are made and the higher the money supply goes. This **recursive relationship between real estate and money supply as well as how they propel each other higher has been detailed in this** .

Self Perpetuating Money Supply

The modern system of real estate investing creates a situation where in real estate catapults the money supply available in the system. This increased money supply then finds its way once again into the real estate sector. This never ending back and forth between the banking system and the real estate system creates an environment of rising real estate prices.

Since the fundamentals of the economy i.e. income levels are not changing, these rising prices are often a real estate bubble. This bubble bursts bringing the prices down for a short period of time. However, in the long run, due to the very nature of the process, real estate investments end up propping up the money supply and creating a self-enforcing and amplifying loop.

Mortgages Create Money

About 80% of the house purchases across the developed nations in the world take place on borrowed money. Hence, the term "house purchase" can be considered to be synonymous with the word "mortgage". This seems to be a normal thing until one considers how the modern banking system works.

Banks do not lend out existing money, instead they create new money when they make loans. Therefore, whenever a bank makes a mortgage loan, it ends up creating that money and pumping it into the system. Therefore, the more mortgages there are, the more money there will be in the system.. This fact can be easily empirically verified by comparing the growth of mortgage loans in the banking industry to the amount of money supply in the economy. The two charts almost move simultaneously!

Money Creates High Inflation

Now, the problem with more money getting created is the fact that this newly created money revolves in the system. It derives its value by reducing the value of the other money in circulation. Therefore, in countries like the United States when the mortgage markets were booming, there was extremely high inflation in the market. The high inflation coupled with mediocre wages growth creates a scenario wherein the workers are losing real wages!

Inflation Creates High Prices

The money that was created as a result of the mortgages finds its way largely into the real estate sector once again. This is because increasing demand for real estate takes the prices higher causing buyers to queue up to buy what appear to be "profitable investments"

Now, excess money as well as excess demand in the system leads to the growth in the prices of real estate units. This further increases investor confidence that real estate is indeed an extremely profitable investment. The real estate prices which initially appeared to be disproportionately high given the economic fundamentals stay that way and the illusion begins to turn into reality! The inflated real estate prices become the new normal.

Speculation Creates More Mortgages

When speculators observe that some of their peers have made money by speculating on real estate, they too make an attempt to join the party. This further exerts an upward pressure on the real estate sector as excess money and excess demand now meet speculative intentions!

This is the perfect recipe for a bubble. Speculators drive the prices sky high through self reinforcing feedback loops. Higher prices in the past become the justification for even higher prices in the future! This period witnesses a rapid growth in mortgages as well as housing prices.

The Bust Phase

Finally, at an unpredictable point in time, the bubble bursts. The primary reason behind the bust is the unsustainable economic condition in the economy. At this point in time, many borrowers are simply unable to make payments to their banks. As a result, the bank has to foreclose these homes and write down the losses. However, very few people know the fact that when banks write down these losses, they actually write the money out of existence. Since mortgages were what created the money in the first place, when these mortgages cease to exist so does the money. As a result, the total money supply in the system is reduced and as a result the prices appear to have gone down.

Thus, mortgages and real estate prices have a huge influence on the money supply of the economy. Since money supply is one of the fundamental economic parameters, the real estate prices end up having a huge influence on the entire economy.

Basic Ratio Analysis of Real Estate Investing

Real estate investing is a sophisticated business. There are sophisticated techniques that are used by many diligent investors to carry out their due diligence. One such sophisticated technique is called ratio analysis. This technique is very similar to the ratio analysis that is carried out while evaluating the financial statements of publically listed corporations. However, there are certain idiosyncrasies and terms that are used only in real estate investments that form a part of this ratio analysis too. **This explains the real estate investment focused ratio analysis from an individual's point of view i.e. what should one person look at when they focus on buying a rental property**. Here are some of the most commonly used ratios.

Loan to Value Ratio

At an individual level, the loan to value (LTV) ratio is probably one of the most important number that is looked at by both banks as well as investors. Both these stakeholders look at the same number for very different reasons.

For instance, the bank looks at the loan to value ratio for the purpose of the security of its own investment. Consider for instance, a property with a loan to value ratio of 90% i.e. if the value of the property is $100, then the bank has financed $90 and has a claim on the property. Now, if the value of the property falls down by 10%, the value of the bank's investment is still secure. The bank therefore provides better interest rates and other terms when the loan to value ratio is lower.

Individuals also look at the loan to value ratio to find the degree of leverage that they are taking on while buying a property. A higher loan to value ratio signifies a risky investment since even a small movement in the property prices would make the investment go in the red.

Debt to Income Ratio

This ratio is used by individuals when they buy real estate for personal use i.e. for personal consumption or investment. The debt to income ratio basically predicts the ease with which a person will be able to make mortgage loan payments.

For instance, it is widely recognized that mortgage payments should form no more than 33% of a person's monthly income. If the mortgage payments are greater than 33%, then the person is at risk of falling under financial duress.

This number is obtained by calculating the annual mortgage payments and then dividing the same by the person's net annual income. To convert the number into a percentage, we can multiply it by 100. If the number is greater than 33%, then the risk is high.

Gross and Net Income Multipliers

This number is used to calculate the amount of dollars that a person is paying as capital investment to gain control of an annual rental value. So, for instance, if this number is 18, then an investor is paying $18 upfront, to gain control of an annual income of $1 in subsequent periods.

This number is calculated by using the market value of the property in the numerator. In the denominator, one can use the gross rental income generated or the net rental income generated after subtracting all the taxes and expenses.

If we use the gross income in the denominator, we get the gross income multiplier whereas if we use the net income in the denominator, we get the net income multiplier.

Rental Yield

The rental yield is a number which is calculated like we calculate the bond yield in the bond markets. The annual rent generated by the property is used in the numerator. Usually, the gross rental value is used in the numerator and no deductions are carried out. However, there are no fixed rules to ratio calculations and every investor calculates the ratios based on their own heuristics.

In the denominator, the price paid for the property is used. Notice that the price paid for the property may be different from its current market value. An investor may have bought the property for $100 and now it may be worth $135. However, we will use the $100 figure. The reason behind this is simple. Yield can only be calculated once the value of your investment is considered. This is not a notional figure. Rather it tells us the exact Return on Investment (ROI) that a buyer is currently obtaining on their property.

Capitalization Rate

The capitalization rate is similar to the rental yield number. However, there is one important difference. The rental yield uses the gross rental income in the numerator. However, the capitalization rate ratio uses the net income i.e. the income that is generated after deducting all operating expenses and taxes from the rental income that is generated by the property. The denominator remains the same i.e. the price that the investor has paid for the property. Once again, the price will not fluctuate based on the market value of the property since this number is not a notional calculation of opportunity costs. Rather, it is the factual calculation of the return on investment on a given property.

The list of ratios that can be used to evaluate a property can never be exhaustive. Ratio analysis is an art and every individual investor uses it in a different way. However, as a general thumb rule, one must remember that real estate investing is largely a cash flow management business and that investors must focus on their ability to generate and sustain predictably increasing cash flows.

Transaction Costs in the Real Estate Market

Flipping properties may sound like a good idea to the novice real estate investor. However, anyone who has even engaged in real estate transactions even once or twice knows that there are significant costs associated with real estate transactions. These costs are called "transaction costs" because they are triggered when a real estate transaction takes place.

These costs tend to be significant and have the potential to burn a hole in your budget if they are not accounted for well in advance. We have listed down some of the common transaction costs. **This**

list is not exhaustive as transaction costs can vary depending on when and where the transaction is taking place. However, they do provide a good understanding of the types of costs that one can expect to incur.

Brokerage

Brokerage is one of the most known costs associated with real estate transactions. This cost is typically a charge by a broker. The job of the broker is to make the buyer and the seller meet. The broker also has to assist during the period of negotiations and convey the offers and counter offers between the buyers and sellers. The broker has to ensure that both the buyer and the seller are on the same page. To do so, they charge a fixed percentage of the transaction value from both the parties.

This model of charging a percentage value from both the parties has come under criticism. This is because this model creates a misalignment between the incentives of the principals to the party and the agent.

Since the broker's compensation is a percentage of the transaction value, the broker has an incentive to maximize the transaction value to maximize their gain!

Search Costs

Search costs are another commonly known cost that are associated with real estate investing. These costs include money paid to newspapers and magazines to advertise the property. Nowadays, online portals allow sellers to advertise their properties for free. However, serious sellers use the premium paid services offered by these websites. Hence, there may be a cost attached with that too. Apart from that if the owner of the house wants to rent the property instead of selling it, there may be costs associated with conducting a credit check of the potential tenant to determine the credit worthiness of the potential tenant.

Apart from that, from the buyer's point of view, visits have to be scheduled to various houses. These visits cost time as well as money and add to the search costs from the buyer's point of view.

Legal and Administrative Costs

The real estate business requires extensive paperwork. This is because the costs of real estate are extremely high. Therefore when any person transacts i.e. buys or sells real estate, they want to ensure that the deal which has been agreed on in person also finds its way to an agreement in black and white. As such, attorneys and lawyers have to be engaged in the process. In fact, real estate transactions tend to be complicated. This is the reason that there are attorneys that specialize in real estate laws.

Also, there are administrative costs involved with the transfer of title for utilities such as water, electricity, cable etc. These transfers take a small but significant amount of time and money too!

Statutory Costs

Across the world, whenever real estate transactions take place, the government usually adds to the transaction costs by taking a portion of the sale proceeds. Across the United Kingdom, Australia, India and in some states in the United States, a stamp duty is levied on the transaction value. Thus, if the transaction was completed for $100, then $3 is owed to the government for the transaction to be considered legally valid! This often results in people undervaluing their transactions on paper and offering black money to the seller, thereby reducing the amount of stamp duty payable.

In many other countries, conveyance of the property title needs to be done by the government. As such, the government charges a hefty conveyance fee. Also many jurisdictions charge another tax called the ad-valorem tax when real estate transactions take place. This obviously is another form of transaction costs being charged by the government.

The statutory costs of real estate transactions are huge and the most visible component of the expenses incurred during the period. As such, they are also the biggest deterrent to buyers and sellers as they make flipping properties difficult as well as expensive.

Financing Costs

Most of the housing transactions that are conducted nowadays are financed using borrowed money. As a result, there are some transaction charges that need to be paid to the lender as well. Consider for instance, the processing fee that is charged by most lenders to process the mortgage agreement. This charge is also a substantial sum usually accounting for 0.15% to 0.25% of the property value. This is the fee charged by lenders for the cost of collecting your documents and running a credit check on them to determine your creditworthiness. Also, this covers the charge of the procedure of loan disbursement that needs to be followed. Apart from the lenders also charge various fees to verify the title of the property in question and for a variety of other services that they provide.

The costs of transacting in real estate are many and varied. This is what makes real estate investment a long term game. Flipping houses like one can flip stocks or bonds is simply not possible because of the complexity of the transaction costs involved.

Information Asymmetry in the Real Estate Market

Successful investors know that it is not the asset class that makes one rich. Rather it is information about the asset class that makes one rich. Therefore, if any investor were to consistently have access to information which is not available in the market, they could trade off of it and gain a handsome return in the process.

The real estate market has one of the most opaque information systems. **Relevant information is not publically disbursed through official sources. Rather, it spreads via grapevine. Therefore, one needs to be well connected to obtain such information and benefit from it**. We have listed the various levels of information that buyers can expect to have.

Level 0 Information: Publically Available

The real estate market does not have near perfect information systems like the stock market or the bond market. This is partly due to the diverse nature of the commodity being traded. The stock and bond markets sell homogenous and standard commodities and as a result can report information which is accurate and enables decision making.

On the other hand, real estate is diverse. Buyers have to consider a wide variety of factors such as location, proximity to daily amenities, neighborhood profile and so on. As a result, the publically available information is imperfect. For instance, if you were to enquire about the prices of property in a completely new neighborhood, odds are that the online and newspaper advertisements will quote a higher price. As you dig deeper into the market and become more familiar with it, you may be able to obtain a better price.

To sum it up, the price discovery mechanism in real estate markets is not efficient. As a result, the publically available information is not very useful when it comes to decision making.

Level 1 Information: Hands on Information

The next level of information is obtained when a buyer actually visits the micro market that he/she is interested in buying a property in. Newspapers and magazines can provide you with a base rate or a range within which the prices should ideally lie. This information is obtained by talking to people who have actually been involved in such deals in the recent past. They can provide a best estimate of the condition of the market as well as the sentiment of buyers and sellers. This information is more valuable than the one which is available through impersonal mediums such as net surfing. As such, more effort has to be spent in collecting it.

Level 2 Information: Available With Mediators

The next level of information is available with the mediators in the market. A buyer can only gather a certain level of information even if he/she visits the micro market on a regular basis before closing in on the deal. This is because they will not be able to witness the closing of multiple deals in the neighborhood.

The deals that are initially floated in the media are very different from the deals which actually go through after negotiations. The mediators have access to both these types of information. They know the details of the advertisements that are displayed in the newspaper as well as the real deals which

Level 3 Information: Available With Bureaucrats

At this stage, we are not talking about information that already exists in the market. Instead, we are talking about future information that may have an effect on the economic value of the property. This may include information such as future development plans or infrastructure plans in and around the neighborhood. For instance, if a new airport were being constructed 5 miles away from your property, it would definitely being more appreciation to you!

This kind of information is not available with the general population. However, law makers and bureaucrats do have access to this information before it is made public. After all, they are the ones that are making these laws. Hence, it is likely that these people who have an unfair information advantage can use this information to their benefit. This usually happens as bureaucrats and law makers pass this information on to their cronies. The cronies then buy up land at the prevailing prices and soon when the information has been made public, they sell their land and the cronies as well as their principal end up making a handsome return.

This kind of information is also called insider information. If it were proved that a person was investing on the basis of such information or even had access to such information, they could be looking at time in prison!

Thus, there are various levels of information available in the market. The amount of money that an investor puts in the market as well the amount of risk that is taken should largely depend on the kind of information that is available. The better the information, the more risk can be taken without suffering too many adverse consequences.

The True Cost of Owning a Property

Home ownership is often considered by the layman as being a single expense i.e. the purchase price of the property. However, if we were to truly analyze the situation, home ownership consists of several expenses. It is easy to forget about some of the expenses while budgeting. Therefore **in this discussion we have prepared a checklist of some of the expenses that usually arise in such scenarios. Some of the investments are as follows:**

Purchase Price

This is the most obvious cost that is associated with real estate investing. Therefore, if we buy a $100000 home, we think that we have invested only that amount. When people ask, "How much did you buy it for?" we give the above figure as the answer. However, as we shall discover in the course of this discussion that the layman's viewpoint that $100000 is the complete cost of the property is usually incorrect.

To begin with there are transaction costs that are associated with the purchase. The transaction costs include brokerage paid, processing fees paid to the bank to process the mortgage loan as well the legal charges that are collected by the government to register the property in the name of the new buyer. First time buyers have a tendency to underestimate these expenses. However, they can quickly climb up to anywhere between 3% and 5% of the property value. Thus, even if the list price of the property is

$100000, the actual price paid by the buyer will be at least $105000!

Interest Paid

Most properties that are purchased today are purchased using borrowed money. Mortgage is the new norm! People buying properties with cash down are virtually unheard of today. However, whenever there is a mortgage, there are mortgage payments and mortgage payments also include an interest component.

The amortization schedule of any mortgage is such that the banks collect all the interest first and then later collect the principal outstanding. For instance if your monthly payment is $1000, then in the first few months $900 will go towards interest itself! In fact, during the first 5 years of servicing a mortgage loan, the borrowers are servicing the interest payments only! Very little principal is reduced during this period. Hence, if these expenses are capitalized i.e.

added to the value of the property, then the value of $100000 goes way above $100000.

Notional Interest

Apart from the interest paid, which is an out of pocket expense for the buyers, there is also notional interest involved in case of real estate investing. Most real estate investments require the buyer to put a down payment on the property. This down payment is close to 10% to 15% of the property value. Thus, for a $100000, a person has to offer an upfront payment of $15000. Now, there is an opportunity cost in making this payment. If this money was not used to make the down payment, then it would be earning interest in a bank or in some other investment. However, once it is used to make the down payment, it earns no interest!

Therefore the amount of notional interest lost should also be added to the property value i.e. to the $100000 that the buyer initially considered was their total investment in the property.

Insurance

Most mortgage lenders require the buyer to have insurance on the property. This is because in the event of natural disasters like earthquakes and hurricanes, the property could be destroyed. As such, the borrower will simply stop making payments towards the property. Therefore, in order to protect their interests, the lenders insist on insurance.

Even apart from the insurance which covers the value of the house, many homeowners opt for insurance for home contents as well. This is because they spend a significant amount of money doing interiors as well as need to make sure that their investment is protected in the event of an unforeseen scenario. This too adds to the cost of property ownership.

Property Taxes

When we buy real estate, we agree to make a stream of payments to the government every year until perpetuity! These payments are called property taxes and almost every government in the world levies these taxes. Once again, these taxes contribute significantly to the cost of home ownership. Also, one needs to understand that these costs are often adjusted in value over time. Therefore, these costs rise with inflation often at the same rate. Hence, while budgeting for buying property one must take into account the costs involved.

Maintenance

Properties across the world now come with amenities. Gated communities with swimming pools and jogging tracks are common. The idea is to provide the people with a lifestyle and not merely with a home. However, these amenities require a lot of maintenance. Gated communities require scores of employees and equipment to guard the place and keep it clean. As such, these charges are also billed to the homebuyers as a monthly expense. This too raises the cost of investment in a property. These costs can sneak up on an unsuspecting buyer and therefore one needs to be extremely wary of the same.

Utilities and Furniture

There are small costs involved with getting the utilities transferred to one's name as well as furnishing the house. These costs too add to the total cost of home ownership.

Home ownership is therefore a complex maze of multiple costs. One needs to be very careful in understanding and budgeting for these hidden expenses as omission of these expenses can significantly dent your budget in the future.

Real Estate Investing vs Investing For Cash Flows

Different types of investors invest in real estate for various reasons. Two of the most common reasons are investing to generate a steady stream of income i.e. cash flows and investing to make a quick buck because of the price rise in the market. This discussion compares both these approaches and the risks and rewards inherent in them.

Investing For Capital Gains vs. Investing For Cash Flow

- **Predictability:** Investing for cash flow has the advantage of being a lot more predictable as compared to investing for capital gain. Buyers who invest for capital gain have very little realistic basis to predict the profits that they expect to make. A lot of these buyers believe that the macro-economic fundamentals of the economy will ensure that the prices continue to rise perpetually! This has not, is not and will not be true of any economy. Real estate industry, like any industry faces cycles of escalating and falling housing prices. Some other home buyers simply believe in the greater fool theory. They simply expect that they will find someone else who will be willing to buy the property from them at an even more inflated price hoping to repeat the same feat that they have accomplished! Therefore, investing for capital gains is largely a buy and hold strategy.

Investing for cash flow on the other hand has the component of predictability. Investors who invest for capital gain have a reasonable idea of the events that are about to unfold. Therefore, they can predict, with a fair deal of certainty, the amount of profit expected on a periodic as well as a long term basis.

- **Sustainability:** Investing for cash flows is more sustainable as compared to investing for capital gains. This is because a cash flow based strategy is grounded in reality. There is cash coming in every month. The cash may be more or less than expected. However, in a well structured deal, there is enough cash to at least cover the operating expenses. This makes the property self sustaining as it can continue to function without any financial support from the investor. This gives the investors more flexibility to manage these properties even when the markets depict a bearish trend.

Properties purchased with an intention of capital gain are markedly different from this. These properties bleed red ink from the very first day. The investors are expected to pump in more and more money during the duration of the property investment. There is a cash inflow only when the investment is terminated i.e. when the property is sold. Hence, if a favorable exit point does not come, investors may run out of cash required to sustain the profit and may have to sell the property at whatever price is being quoted in the market. Such distressed sales make investing for capital gains an unviable proposition.

- **Tax Efficient:** Investing for cash flows is far more tax efficient than investing for capital gains. The capital gain laws in most countries make it impossible to flip properties without incurring a serious loss in the form of taxation.

Rental income which forms the core of any strategy based on cash flow has significant tax advantages. Investors are allowed to deduct a wide range of expenses from the rental income. Therefore, they can significantly lower their income and pay lowered taxes based on their lowered income. Also, since rental income accrues over many years, it gets spread out and hence is taxed at a lower rate.

On other hand, capital gains appear in one shot as an income. This takes the income of the investor in a higher tax bracket and as such they are taxed at a higher rate. There are some deductions available when investors book capital gains from a given property. However, these deductions are nowhere as efficient in reducing income as compared to deductions available when the property is rented out.

- **Riskiness:** If we simply define risk as a measure of deviation from the norm, investing for capital gains is far more risky as compared to investing for cash flows. Capital values tend to fluctuate a lot in the real estate sector. However, if we look at the rental values, they show a predictable appreciation of 8%-10% per year. Therefore, there is less volatility in the rental market. Any investment that is made based on cash flow projections of the rental market is less risky as compared to investments made based on future capital values.

Also, investors have a higher degree of control over the rental values than they have on the capital values. Investors can make property improvements and significantly improve the rental prospects of a given property. The same cannot be said regarding the capital value of a given property.

Opportunities in Bear Markets

Properties which produce positive cash flows are not easily available. They are certainly not advertised on the first page of your daily newspaper. These properties are found after hunting for a bargain for a significant amount of time. Also, these bargains are found in bear markets such as the one that was present in 2008 sub prime crisis. During this period, more and more people face foreclosure. Therefore these people do not have homes as their homes are being sold in the market for cheap. On the other hand, these families want to rent apartments so that they can live in them. Therefore the rental values remain strong or even go up despite depreciating capital values!

It is in such rare times that sophisticated real estate investors ensure that they have the cash on hand to make deals and buy properties which provide a predictable stream of cash flow to the buyers!

Real Estate Investment Trusts (REITs)

Real Estate Investment Trusts (REITs) have become the buzzword when it comes to investing in real estate. They have provided above average returns in countries like the United States where they were first implemented. This has led to the growing popularity of the Real Estate Investment Trusts (REITs) and today more countries in the world are adopting this investment structure. In this discussion, we will explain in detail what Real Estate Investment Trusts (REITs) means and why they provide a more beneficial way to invest in real estate than other legal structures.

Concept of Real Estate Investment Trusts (REITs)

About five decades ago, the concept of Real Estate Investment Trusts (REITs) was first introduced in the United States. Ever since, this idea has grown tremendously in terms of market acceptance. REITs have gone from being an alternative investment class to being an investment class that has become the choice of the majority.

The concept of REITs is simple. Just like a mutual fund allows investors to benefit from

diversification and professional expertise of the fund managers, so do these trusts. These trusts pool in the money collected from a lot of investors. Then they use money from this pool to invest long term in properties. However, the individual investor need not be in for a long term investment. Real Estate Investment Trusts (REITs) have a secondary market. Therefore, any individual investor call sell their share of the investment to other investors in the market at the ongoing price.

Since prices for shares of Real Estate Investment Trusts are quoted on a real time basis, these trusts provide the individual investor with much needed liquidity that is usually absent when one makes real estate investments.

Buying Real Estate Investment Trusts (REITs) is buying a Business

REITs invest the money that they have collected in real estate. However, it would be incorrect to assume that Real Estate Investment Trusts are nothing more than a vehicle for secondary investments in realty. In reality, investing in Real Estate Investment Trusts (REITs) is like investing in a business.

This means that if two Real Estate Investment Trusts are given the exact same amount of money, they will end up making very different returns based on how they are managed. In fact, if they are given the exact same properties to manage, the returns would still be pretty different! Hence, the returns provided by Real Estate Investment Trusts (REITs) depend more on their management expertise and style than other factors. Therefore, buying a share in Real Estate Investment Trusts (REITs) is equivalent to buying shares in a business.

History

Real Estate Investment Trusts started in 1960's in the United States wherein they were amateur investments. President Eisenhower had signed the REIT Act into existence. The idea was to provide the average investor the benefit of investing in commercial properties. Prior to REITs such investments were only available to huge financial institutions and extremely wealthy individuals. With the advent of REITs, the masses could now have access to the same investments!

The idea of Real Estate Investment Trusts (REITs) became extremely popular in the United States as multiple legislations were created in the future to enable efficient functioning of these trusts. The idea then became so successful that today it has spread worldwide. Many countries such as Malaysia, Australia, Hong Kong and even developing nations like Ghana have embraced the concept of Real Estate Investment Trusts.

Specialization

One of the biggest changes that have happened in the Real Estate Investment Trusts (REITs) space is that the industry has become highly specialized. When the industry first came into existence, the trust would buy pretty much any property that they could get their hands on. For instance, they would buy commercial office space, malls and even multi-property residential homes. However, over time, the industry realized that the risk reward profiles of each of these investments are different. As such, companies started specializing in one of these property types. Today, most Real Estate Investment Trusts (REITs) will exclusively state the type of property that they invest in and the risk rewards that accrue as a result in their investment brochure. Investors therefore have more control over where their money is being invested.

Future

At the present moment, the short term future of the Real Estate Investment Trusts (REITs) is considered to be negative. This is because the Fed is about to announce its QE tapering program. QE tapering is expected to hit all asset classes. However, one of the worst hit is going to be real estate. After all, real estate has been the source at which the entire crisis which led to QE and QE tapering started.

The Real Estate Investment Trusts (REITs) arc therefore expected to see a period of turmoil in the forthcoming years. However, the long term outlook on real estate seems good. Since, Real Estate Investment Trusts are one of the best ways to invest in real estate the long term outlook on REITs seems good by extension.

Advantages to Investing in Real Estate Investment Trusts

In the last, we studies about what Real Estate Investment Trusts (REITs) are. We also understood that they have become remarkably popular in a very short span of time and that they have a place in virtually every portfolio in the United States. We also learned that this trend is fast spreading across the globe.

However, we did not fundamentally understand the factors that were underlying this Real Estate

Investment Trust (REIT) boom. we have listed down some of the factors which make investing in these trusts lucrative and profitable! The advantages to investing in Real Estate Investment Trusts (REITs) are as follows:

Liquidity

Liquidity is the foremost reason that anyone would want to invest in REITs. Real estate as an asset class is known to have a good risk return profile. This means that it provides great returns and the risk of downside is not as high when compared to other investments. However, real estate as an asset class has a significant drawback which is that it is highly illiquid. Investors who want to cash out on their real estate investments have to wait for weeks (if not months) to do so. This is where investing in Real Estate Investment Trusts (REITs) comes to the rescue. The securities sold by REITs are listed on many exchanges across the world. As such they can be bought and sold like shares of a blue chip corporation! Therefore investors who put their money in Real Estate Investment Trusts (REITs) get the benefit of extremely high liquidity which was virtually unheard of in the real estate market.

Diversification

REITs provide the opportunity for diversification to small ticket real estate investors. Real estate investments require a significant financial commitment on the behalf of the buyer. As such, investors can only invest in a few places. Therefore, they are exposed to the risks and returns of those micro-markets. Anyone familiar with investing knows that putting all your eggs in one basket is a dangerous proposition. This is the reason many people believe that real estate is an extremely risky proposition.

However, Real Estate Investment Trusts provide an opportunity to diversify this risk. This is because these trusts own a wide variety of properties. They own apartments, condos, offices, retail establishment etc and they own these properties in different markets. As such, they have sufficient diversification to protect themselves from the risks any one micro-market may present. This is what has made REITs a preferred choice for many investors.

Choice

REITs provide a lot of choice to individual investors. There are various types of trusts which are catering to the needs of diverse investors. There are some Real Estate Investment Trusts (REITs) which invest exclusively in equity. This means that they buy the properties outright and therefore gain from the cash flows and capital appreciation that these properties provide in the long term. Their returns however are variable and are subject to the vagaries of the market. On the other hand, Real Estate Investment Trusts (REITs) also offer a debt based investment opportunity. Such funds loan out to real estate developers. These developers then pay a fixed return on the loans which is passed on the investors of the fund. Therefore, Real Estate Investment Trusts have opportunities for risky as well as risk averse investors. By buying a combination of debt and equity based REITs one can create any risk-reward portfolio which is to their liking!

Predictability

Real Estate Investment Trusts provide a lot of predictability compared to other investments. The underlying investment made by REITs is in real estate. Real estate as an asset class has a very predictable rate of appreciation as well as rates at which rentals grow. Therefore, the cash flows from such a fund can be predicted with a high degree of accuracy and certainty. Most Real Estate Investment Trusts (REITs) in the United States confirm to analyst projections of their revenues and expenses year after year. This has given analysts the confidence that they can predict the cash flows with a high degree of confidence.

If the records for the past few years are considered, Real Estate Investment Trusts (REITs) have consistently outperformed the stock markets and they have done so with a high degree of certainty. Less volatility and higher returns makes REITs a favorite!

Professional Management

Lastly, Real Estate Investment Trusts are businesses that are run by well qualified professional investors. As such, they have their methodologies in place and make decisions based on them. It is highly unlikely that the management of Real Estate Investment Trusts makes erroneous decisions regarding managing any given property. This professional management is worth a lot of money and individual investors would simply not be able to afford it and the increased cash flow that it brings to the table. Since a lot of investors pool in money and each of them only has to pay a slice of the management fee, they can benefit from the financial and operational expertise that many of these real estate investors bring to the table.

How To Predict Real Estate Market and Identify Asset Bubbles ?

Housing prices can go up under two main scenarios:

1. One is when the fundamental economy of a given location has undergone a change. This means that there is somehow a better standard of living or more employment available in that area making it imperative for more people to stay there.

2. Or else, there could be a speculative bubble wherein investors buy at a high price today to be able to sell at an even higher price tomorrow.

The question arises as to how can one predict the markets ? **How can one differentiate the realistic price rise from the bubbles ?** we will make an attempt to explain some of the metrics that can allow the investors to do so.

Interest Rates

Interest rates have been the common factor in every boom and bust scenario that we have witnessed in the property market. Whether or not, they are the direct cause is a question of debate. However, they are definitely amongst one of the causes.

All the property market booms, be it in Japan, United States, China or India, have been perpetuated in an atmosphere of low interest rates. This is because low interest rates lead to excess money supply and a scenario wherein the buyers are suddenly flush with excess cash and queuing up to buy homes.

The converse of this is also true. All the downfalls in the property market have also been created by a sudden and unexpected increase in interest rates. All the crises right from the subprime mortgage crises to the "lost decade" all have their roots in the rising interest rates.

As an investor, **one should therefore stay away from any markets where the rise in property**

prices seems to be fuelled by a dropping interest rate. This is because, in most scenarios, this is likely to be a property bubble.

Housing Inventory

Another important metric that real estate investors can gauge to judge whether or not a market is in a bubble state is the housing inventory. Housing inventory indicates the amount of unsold homes that the developers have in a given market.

In the usual market scenario, the housing inventory in a market remains stable. This is because developers have a rough idea of the number of homes that buyers will purchase in a given period and will therefore create houses that can fulfill that demand without leading to excess supply. However, when a bull market is approaching, there is suddenly a shortage in housing inventory. This means that there will be no homes available in the market! On the other hand, during a bear market, there is a sudden increase in the housing inventory. Therefore, there are multiple homes available in the market. However, very few buyers are willing to purchase them.

Thus, keeping an eye on the housing inventory number can tell an investor, what stage of the business cycle is the market currently in?

Absorption Rates

Absorption rates are like the opposite of housing inventory. Housing inventory tells us the number of unsold homes in a market during a given period. On the other hand, absorption rates tell us the number of homes that have been purchased in the market during a given period. This number can be usually estimated from the number of requests received by the government for transfer of property titles. Once again, a rising number signifies a bull run and a falling number signifies a bear run.

Wages to Capital Values

Another measure of affordability is to compare the annual wages of an average person who stays in a given neighborhood with the capital values that are prevalent in the neighborhood. The result will give us the number of years that a person will have to work in order to buy a house in a given area. The average wages are usually estimated from the median wages of the workers living in a given area.

Numbers between the ranges of 5 to 10 signify affordability. This is because if a person can buy a house with 100% of their wages in 5 to 10 years, they can afford one on a 20 year mortgage. However, if the number goes beyond 20, it signifies a bubble.

The underlying roots of this high price could be the fact that it is an investor driven market and the average person is just a tenant!

Rental to Capital Values

One of the best ways to predict a housing bubble is to compare the rental values to the capital values. When the underlying economic fundamentals of a given property change, the rental as well as capital values change simultaneously.

However, in the event of a bubble, speculators raise the capital values expecting even more capital gain. However, the rental values do not rise because the tenants do not see a change in the value of the property. Therefore, in such markets there is a huge disparity between rental and capital values which can be considered to be the sure shot sign of a bubble.

Thus, there are various indicators in the property market that can help the diligent investor differentiate between a price rise and an asset bubble.

Japanese Real Estate Market

The Japanese real estate story is important as well as different. Most property market stories that one would hear include periods of booms and busts. The property market goes under for a few years only to recover a few years later. However, the case of Japan has been very different. The Japanese market witnessed a bull run never witnessed before. This period continued till 1991.

Then came the downfall! Since 1991, Japan has witnessed a downfall of epic proportions. The property valuations have significantly fallen and have stayed there for over two decades despite the frantic efforts of the Japanese government to revive it.

We will witness the story of the Japanese crash, the implications of which are still seen in the Japanese market.

Three Decades Long Economic Miracle

After World War-2, the Japanese economy was virtually destroyed. They had been fighting battles for decades and as such their economy had suffered a lot. Also, two of their major cities Hiroshima and Nagasaki had been bombed out of existence by the United States. As such the worker morale was also low.

However, the post war economy of Japan experienced an economic boom. Japanese corporations started making major headway in the electronics and automobile markets of the world.

This led to an increased prosperity in the economy. The high prosperity created jobs for many Japanese employees. This along with the fact that Japanese corporations consider employees to be part of their family i.e. never fire them gave rise to an increased purchasing power.

By the late 70's and early 80's, Japan which was a country that had an area smaller than the state of California and was consistently rocked by natural disasters like earthquakes and volcano eruptions had become the second largest economy in the world. It was slowly closing in on the heels of United States. To many economic observers this was nothing short of an economic miracle which Japan had pulled off in three decades.

During these three decades, the Japanese real estate market witnessed a steady upward boom. The prices of real estate were being driven up at around the rate of economic growth and very few suspected any sort of bubble being created.

Tax Laws Modified

Around the mid 1980's the government of Japan decided to liberalize its hitherto conservative property markets. The Japanese property markets had a draconian taxation regime which prevented any change in the ownership of properties. For instance, if a property was sold in less than two years after its purchase, taxes accounted for over 90% of the capital appreciation! If the same property was sold more than two years but less than five years after its purchase, around 75% of the capital gains made by the investors were payable to the Japanese government as tax. If the investors sold the property at any time after 5 years, 50% of the capital appreciation was payable as tax.

In short, the transaction costs of Japanese real estate market made it unviable for anyone else except genuine homebuyers to buy a property. This changed in the mid 80's as the government of Japan revoked a lot of these rules to create an open real estate market to suit the needs of the open Japanese economy.

Stock Market and Real Estate Market Loop

As a result of the economic miracle and the liberalized laws pertaining to real estate, a situation was created wherein the real estate and the stock market started feeding off each other. Many people would sell off their highly valued stocks in the market to buy real estate. This created a demand for real estate that was rising in value. As such, many real estate investors would cash out and then once again buy stocks of Japanese corporations. Both these asset classes in the Japanese markets were outperforming every other investment in the world. As such, they attracted more and more money and the valuation of both these asset classes went sky high! By 1991, real estate valuations in Tokyo were several times higher than competing valuations in more prosperous cities like New York and London.

The 90's: Real Estate Crash

The 90's marked the beginning of the end for the real estate market in Japan. The Bank of Japan raised interest rates drastically to curb the inflation that was caused by the loose monetary policy that it had followed for decades. As a result of this raised interest rates, money supply in the market became tight. Also the mortgages became more expensive to service. Therefore, the demand for Japanese real estate suddenly went down. This created the ultimate downward spiral as property prices ended up plunging more than 64% in Japan in the short period of a decade! Investors and homeowners, most of whom, were highly leveraged, lost a significant portion of their investments as prices continued to crumble.

2015: Worth Half the Price!

Today, in 2015, the Japanese housing market has still not recovered. This is after the fact that Japan has held its interest rates near zero percent for many years now. On top of that Japan has also followed a quantitative easing program but that too has proved to be ineffective in raising the prices of the real estate market once again.

Today, the average price of real estate in Japan is over a 50% discount compared to the peak prices that were seen in 1991. The prices are approximately at a level when they were in 1985 i.e. when the bubble had just begun.

To sum it up, **if you had invested in Japanese real estate in 1985 and wanted to cash out after three decades, you would have ZERO capital appreciation!** This is what makes the Japanese real estate story important as well as interesting for any student or real estate investor.

The American Real Estate Market

The United States of America is one of the most developed countries in the world. It is also known for having the most transparent market system in the world. Since many economies in the world as so integrated with American economies, a movement in the American markets has ripple effects all across the globe.

This fact became more evident in 2007, when a local real estate crisis in the American markets became a crisis of global proportions and threatened to bring the financial system of the world to a grinding halt! The study of real estate markets would therefore not be complete unless the recent history of the American markets is understood. **We will describe the two major boom bust cycles that the American real estate sector has witnessed since the 1980's.**

1. **Stage 1: The Bust**

   The American real estate market was witnessing a bust from the 1980's onwards. This bust was created by the Savings and Loan crisis that was present in the markets during this period. Prior to 1980's, most of the homes being purchased in the United States were being purchased as a result of money borrowed from these Savings and Loans institutions.

However, in the 1980's the Fed realized that inflation was slipping out of control. As a result, Paul Volcker who was leading the Fed at that time increased the interest rates to as much as 20%! This interest rate hike almost wiped out the savings and loan industry as they were not able to attract new capital at these rates. Also, the number of people who would borrow at this rate to buy a home went down significantly bringing a crash in the real estate market.

The savings and loans crisis ended up creating what was then what was one of the lowest points in the history of United States real estate. However, by then the people had no idea as to what was in store for them later!

2. Stage 2: The Manufactured Boom

The 90's were spent recouping from the savings and loan crisis. The savings and loan institutions had become insolvent. However, some of the other financial institutions were also under severe financial duress. Hence lending activity was low. The government enacted various laws to increase the lending and particularly the lending to the real estate sector.

Legislations like the Communities Reinvestment Act were created with the intention of increasing lending to the minority community. Soon, the political motive of the fulfilling the so called "America Dream" took over all rationality. The politicians were adamant on creating policies that would enable more people to buy homes. The long term implications of these policies were simply not thought through.

What followed is known as one of the largest boom periods in American history. This boom was largely enabled by the rock bottom interest rates i.e. close to 1% that was prevalent in the United States at that time. To add to this, banks were instructed by law to lower their lending standards to ensure that they are able to make as many loans as possible!

As a result of all these activities, the real estate market found itself flooded with buyers who suddenly had a lot of money are were willing to buy properties that always seemed to appreciate in value making their owners rich. This boom in the American real estate industry lasting from the late 1990's to 2007 was created as a result of the policies of the American government. As a result, it is often called the manufactured boom.

3. Stage 3: The Crisis

The year 2007 created one of the biggest financial crises that the world had ever seen. This crisis had its roots in the American real estate industry. The manufactured boom that was created as a result of the government policies soon became a manufactured crisis. This is because once again, fearing inflation, President

Alan Greenspan had to raise the interest rates in the economy.

This increase in interest rates created an unprecedented crisis called the subprime mortgage crisis. The increased interest rates led to the monthly payments of mortgages going up. Many homeowners could not afford their increased mortgage. As a result, the houses had to be foreclosed. The declining value of the houses created a scenario of excess supply wherein the prices were contracting even further. During this bloodbath, almost all of the markets in the world were adversely affected. However, the worst hit was the American real estate market which had lost almost half of its value!

4. Stage 4: The Post-Crisis Market

The United States real estate market has been healing post the depression that hit it in 2008. However, the healing has been slow. The drastic drops that were witnessed by the real estate market are now being replaced by a steady rise. However, the good news is that this time, the government intervention in the market is minimal and neither is this moderate growth being driven by insanely low interest rates. There are some critics that point a finger towards the Quantitative Easing policies being followed in the United States for the steady rise. However, nothing can be conclusively said as of now.

To sum it up, the United States real estate sector has a history of ups and downs. Real estate is far from the steadily and predictably rising investment class that many people make it out to be. In fact, it is almost as risky as other investment (if not more)

China's Real Estate Market

The real estate market in China has undergone a complete shift. At one point in time, the Chinese workers were assured of secure housing by their communist government. However, **the recent trend in Chinese real estate has made real estate**

unaffordable even for the highly paid middle class employees making it a completely different ball game.

The situation has therefore completely changed from socialism to capitalism. This drastic change in the Chinese real estate market has been documented in this .

Communism

The Chinese real estate market forms a fascinating tale of the rise of hardcore capitalism in a communist country. In the beginning, i.e. in 1978, Chinese real estate had no price. This was because all the land in the state of China was owned by the government. The Chinese constitution prohibited private ownership and transfer of land.

As such, there could not be any buy or sell transactions. All the employees were also working for the government. Therefore they would be provided housing on the basis of their seniority, number of years of service and size of their family amidst other factors. At this juncture, it would have been impossible to predict that one day China would become one of the biggest real estate markets in the world and would one day be a major example used in debates pertaining to real estate bubbles.

Privatization Takes Over

Things began to slowly change in the socialist economy of China. The economy no longer remained socialist in 1988 when the constitution was amended. Laws which did not allow for private ownership of land were now amended.

The latest laws divided land into two categories:

1. One category was reserved for the people of the lower income households. These houses were to be sold on a cost plus basis. Also, the government would keep a strict check on the costs incurred in building these houses. Developers who created and executed these projects without any hiccups would get tax credits for the same. Ideally these houses were

sold at 5% above the cost price to the low income families.

However, there were restrictive conditions which made it difficult to qualify for such a home. Also, exit from such a home was not easy as the government prohibited selling off these homes for a period of at least 5 years after its purchase.

2. The other types of houses being sold were commodity housing. This was the category of the real estate market that was driven by the markets i.e. investors could freely buy and sell their properties at whatever prices they saw fit. In the meanwhile, they could also rent out these properties. The rent control act of 1994 completed the transformation of a part of Chinese real estate market from socialistic to capitalistic.

Property Boom

The next couple of decades saw one of the biggest property booms that the world has ever witnessed.

The size of the government controlled affordable homes in the economy has been steadily shrinking. Over time, they have been replaced with commodity housing. Even though the supply of commodity houses has greatly increased across Chinese cities, so have their prices.

The average price rise for over two decades has been in double digits every year. This means that the prices of houses have increased by a minimum of eightfold during this twenty year period. In many cities, the averages have been as high as 26% compounded annual growth rate for around two decades! This can be considered to be one of the biggest and longest lasting bull runs in any real estate market across the world. The rapidly rising prices made real estate go out of the reach of working class population. This prompted the Chinese government to once again enact stricter laws.

Strict Laws on Second and Third Home

The Chinese government has enacted strict laws to curb the purchase of second and third homes in most Chinese cities. These laws were enacted to ensure that poor first home borrowers were not facing competition from wealthy second or third home borrowers.

The laws entail that people buying their second home must make a down payment of at least 60% of their property value. Similarly, if the person is buying a third home, they would be provided no financing and would be required to pay the entire amount in cash.

This law had serious repercussions on the housing sales in tier-1 and tier-2 cities. The rapidly rising house prices quickly saw a correction. China thus saw its first real estate bust during this period!

Stimulus Package

In 2008, the Chinese government provided a stimulus package to revive its banking sector and encourage lending. However, this ended up once again increasing the real estate prices which the government had taken so long to subdue. The banks were flush with cash and real estate developers seemed keen on borrowing and as such a lot of money was lent to them at a frantic pace. For a short while, the bust quickly turned into a boom. However, this boom was extremely short lived.

Misallocation

The Chinese developers built huge gated communities and townships. Most of these were built for the higher class people since there is minimum government regulation in that price range. However, the elite class has not purchased these houses. As a result, China now has entire towns and cities which are ready for inhabitation. However, they have not been inhabited. They are commonly referred to as ghost cities by many economists and represent one of the largest misallocation of funds in the history of the centrally managed Chinese economy.

At the present moment, some cities in China are witnessing a downfall in their property prices whereas the prices have stagnated in some other cities. If the market sentiment is to be believed China is about to witness a serious correction of real estate prices.